I0448682

The Energy Puzzle Between the United States and China

Appear at places to which he must hasten; move swiftly where he does not expect you.

—Sun Tzu

China's rapid economic growth over the last three decades has been matched by its greater demand for energy. This expansion involves modernization in four specific areas; agriculture, industry, science and technology, and national defense.[1] China's strategic objectives include: preserving Communist Party rule, sustaining economic growth and development, defending national sovereignty and territorial integrity, achieving national unification, maintaining internal stability, and securing China's status as a great power.[2] As of 2011, China is the second largest consumer of natural resources (oil, liquefied petroleum gas (LPG), kerosene, and coal) in the world, behind the United States. Collectively, the U.S. and China are the two largest oil markets and oil importers and account for 60% of annual world oil demand growth.[3]

This comparison on energy consumption between the U.S. and China sets the potential for a global energy "conflict" between the two countries. A conflict not so much in the traditional sense of an all out armed war, but a conflict over development, demand and supply. Natural resource supply projections for the next 30 years still have oil and coal as the top two fossil fuel consumables. This has lead to countries all around the world to research and develop alternative and reusable energy sources.

To understand the relative size of the U.S. and China's oil consumption as compared to the rest of the world, the chart below depicts the 10 largest oil consuming countries in the world as of 2011. The U.S. measures in at 18, 835 barrels per day while

China is a distant second with approximately half, 9,758. The remaining countries are at or below 4,000 barrels per day.

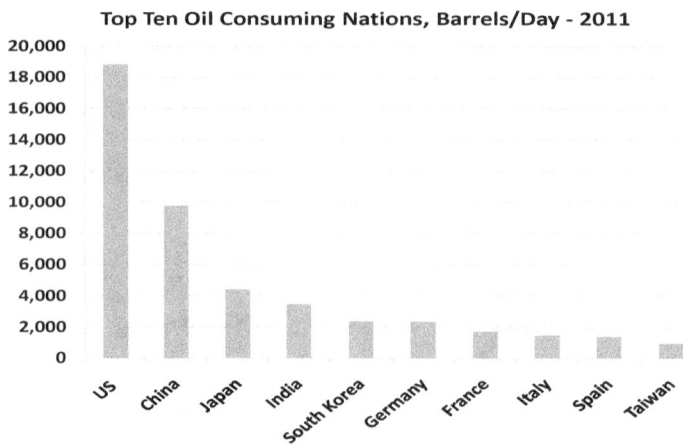

Figure 1. Source: BP Statistical Review of World Energy 2012

In 2011, China's overall consumption of natural resources rose by 5.5% from 2010. Specifically, fuel oil consumption rose 2.5%.[4] Conversely, the U.S. consumption of the same products decreased 1.8%, as fuel oil dropped 10.3% from 2010 to 2011. This trend in the U.S. is based on alternative fuel research, implementation and consumption of other natural resources such as coal and natural gas. This is an area China is still developing. China's consumption of natural resources has doubled from 2000 to 2007.[5] Its trajectory to 2035 is estimated to double again. This accelerated rise in energy consumption poises China to be the number one energy consuming country in the world, which would make it account for more than a quarter of the world's energy consumption by that time.[6]

Based on China's energy requirements and future needs, questions remain about how will China acquire its energy needs for the present and the future? Could China's recent assertiveness in the South China Sea attempting to claim its stakes to oil

2

and gas fields, cause an armed conflict amongst the littoral states or worse, between China and the U.S.? Will this fight for energy among the U.S. and its allies against China break the current fragile relationship the U.S. has with China? If a conflict arises between China and the U.S., what will become of the globally economically entwined nations that rely on the China and U.S. economies? The ultimate question to this puzzle lies in the diplomatic process between the U.S. and China. Can there be cooperation between the two superpowers over the use and sharing of natural resources?

This assessment follows the policy set by Secretary Panetta on June 2, 2012 at the Shangri-La Dialogue in Singapore, "China has a critical role to play in advancing security and prosperity by respecting the rules-based order that has served the region for six decades."[7] China must come to understand its relevance and understand that it must share in the growth and prosperity of all nations worldwide.

The answers to the question posed above could be that; China will acquire/find its energy needs through agreements with Russia (pipelines); Africa, (natural gas development); Iran, (oil imports); China's own natural gas development on the mainland and in the shallow waters in the South China Sea. An armed conflict could occur amongst the littoral states regarding natural gas exploration and claims. However, there are too many hindrances to China prosecuting a full out conflict with these states. Any prolonged conflict between these states would most definitely break any agreements/treaties or alliances and destroy any future for a peaceful existence. The economic environment would also be destroyed.

Since the world's economies are so entwined, any type of an economic sanction would not only hurt China, but the U.S. as well. Diplomacy will have to prevail in the matters dealing with China, the South China Sea and the "fight" over energy. Cooperation appears to be the only feasible solution. China will have to learn how to compromise and become a model player in the international arena.

In order for the answers to the energy dilemma between the U.S. and China to be followed through and cultivated, U.S. policy must shape the rising China and turn it into a responsible world superpower. For China to be "lead" by the U.S., the U.S. must lead by example. U.S. policy must be geared towards diplomatic pursuits.

The State of Energy in the World

The current state of energy in the world today is a precursor to what lies ahead for energy supply and demand for 2030. The demand for all types of energy is based primarily on each country's economy or Gross domestic Product (GDP). While the 2008-2009 global economic crises curtailed energy consumption, the recovery period since then has shown that energy consumption is again on the rise. The graph below depicts energy consumption comparing the countries belonging to the Office of Economic Development (OECD) to those non-OECD countries.

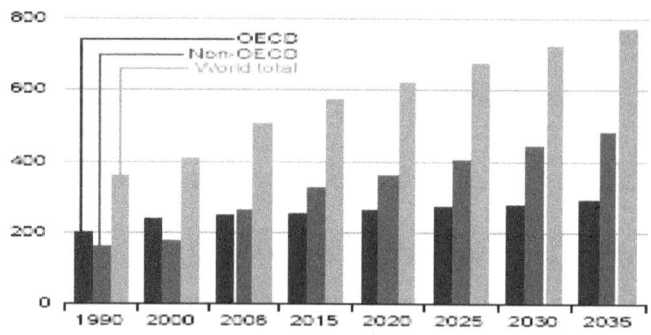

Figure 2. Source: U.S. Energy Information Administration, September 2011

The largest country in the non-OECD category is China. OECD member countries are, for the most part, more advanced energy consumers. Energy demand in the OECD economies grows slowly over the projection period, at an average annual rate of 0.6 percent, whereas energy consumption in the non-OECD emerging economies expands by an average of 2.3/year.[8] The graph also depicts the non-OECD countries eventually consuming more natural resources/energy by 2015 and out to 2035.

This projected trend by the IEA ties in directly with a BP presentation focused on the energy outlook for 2030. The presentation outlined that the world needs more energy and will need to continue produce more energy to meet the needs of each country's economic growth. BP also projected that between 2010 and 2030, overall energy consumption in the world will increase approximately 40%.[9] This has much of the world worried in the sense of, "where is this increased energy requirement and supply going to come from?" The key area BP projected was North America and its energy resources, specifically tight oil and shale gas. The U.S. specifically has become a major exporter of shale gas. This is based on the fact that the U.S. has the right ground conditions that can produce and export the gas. North America, (U.S.) has the free access, wherein competitiveness among companies gives them a chance to develop and use state of the art technology to explore and develop the natural gas deposits.

The key point in the BP report was that North America will become by the year 2030, energy independent, while China and India will become more dependent on energy. They lack the technological, free access of an open capitalist market to explore energy development. With the capitalist system and free enterprise, comes competition, which spurs advanced technologies for natural gas exploration and development. This projected status of the energy picture in the future lays the groundwork for energy cooperation amongst the super powers in the world.

The bottom line is that trends in the energy consumption, supply and demand, exploration are tied into what the current economic conditions exists in the world. Since 2000, China's oil demand growth has been around 5 percent or more.[10] Economics and energy resources are co-dependent. As an example, the U.S.'s interdependence with China's economy is staggering. China is only second to the U.S. in GDP. As of 2010, the U.S. had $2.165 trillion in foreign debt, of which China held $1.95 trillion, with $798 billion in U.S. Treasuries, and exports $270 billion and imports only $61 billion from the U.S.[11] With China's growing economy and need for natural resources to maintain and continue its growth, as well the U.S.'s interdependence with China's economy, these two nations will need to co-exist in the same environments and respect each other's needs.

The global picture of the world's energy situation needs to be narrowed down between the two super powers that control, consume, develop and export the world's energy on a daily basis. China's crude oil imports come from the Middle East at approximately 46 percent and 22 percent is imported from Africa.[12] With China's reliance on Middle Eastern oil, and its contentious environment, the question remains, what action would China take to defend its interests and its alliances with Iran? In the event of a U.S./Iranian conflict, would China intervene and establish a military alliance with Iran? Most likely, this scenario would not evolve into an armed conflict between the three nations. It would have a devastating effect on economic and energy security. Although China is dependent on Iranian oil, it is pursuing other avenues to secure its oil requirements.

The chart below depicts China's overall oil imports from around the world. In 2011, China's biggest importer of oil was Saudi Arabia with Angola and Iran coming in second and third. Of note, Venezuela and Brazil combine to export approximately 354 thousand of barrels per day to China.   To meet its increasing demand in natural resources, China is building alliances around the world, at the same time; the power of the U.S. to shape global energy affairs is eroding[13]. The interpretation of this is that China's rise in the global energy market is growing, quickly. China is forming alliances and treaties with countries that can supply them with resources that are scarce or difficult to extract in and around mainland China.

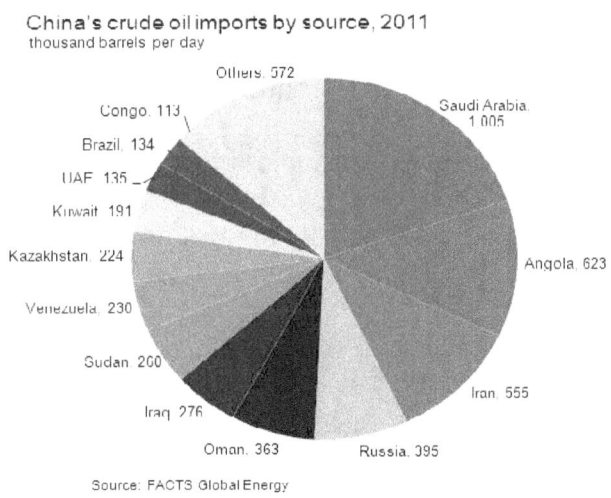

Figure 3. Source: U.S. Energy Information Administration

The expansion of China in its crude oil production and exports with Venezuela and Brazil could either strengthen relations or become a more contentious area with the U.S. Currently, the U.S. receives two thirds of Venezuelan oil.[14] As stated by Secretary

7

of Defense Leon Panetta in June 2012, on the issue of U.S. - China relations, "Our aim is to continue to improve the strategic trust that we must have between our two countries, and to discuss common approaches to dealing with shared security challenges."[15]   Secretary Panetta was describing the Asian Pacific Rim in his comments; the Western Hemisphere is also a viable operational environment where both countries need to share common interests, resources and challenges.

Before there can be further discussion about China and its crude oil requirements, it must be noted that oil is not China's largest energy source, it is coal. Coal supplied the vast majority (70 percent) of China's total energy consumption of 90 quadrillion British thermal units (Btu) in 2009.[16] Fortunately for China, they are the world top producer of coal. China also "burns" other types of energy as well, such as natural gas, nuclear and other renewables, but these make up a small part of its total consumption. Although growth in coal consumption in China likely will slow in the coming decade due to government carbon reduction targets, coal will continue t o dominate China's energy mix in the foreseeable future.[17] With this trend continuing in China and the U.S. becoming less dependent on foreign oil, and the U.S. a major exporter of coal, it is evident to see that cooperation and sharing of energy resources will be in the offing for these two countries.

China's other pursuits of natural resources has lead to many alliances with in the Central Asian states, most notably with Russia. Recently, China and Russia have signed four agreements on energy cooperation. The two countries signed a memorandum of understanding in cooperation on energy market assessment, a roadmap on cooperation in the coal sector, the minutes of the meeting on coal cooperation and an agreement on electricity supply.[18] This memorandum of understanding also includes collaboration to further expand coal and power trade, undertake research on energy reservation and promote the application of renewable energy.[19] This is just another example of China's growth and expansion in its pursuit of energy security and diversification in the pursuit of its energy requirements.

The current state of supply and demand for oil, gas and other natural resources for the U.S. will contrast China's demands and illustrate where the U.S. is heading toward for energy reliance. The U.S. reliance on oil imports has decreased. The decrease is related to many factors, such as higher efficiency vehicles, alternative fuel development and a vast reserve of natural gas and oil reserves. The U.S. is currently transforming its huge coal refining plants into natural gas plants. Basically the conversion to natural shale gas is undercutting coal prices and taking over as the U.S.'s fuel of choice for electric power.[20] This is just a small step for the U.S. in converting to a cleaner cheaper fuel for the future. This conversion to natural gas also underscores BP's comments about the U.S. and more specifically North America becoming energy independent by the year 2030. However, with all of this alternative energy development and use, oil is still the primary fuel consumed by the U.S.

The U.S. imports oil from a geopolitically diverse array of nations: The Persian Gulf, (roughly 10%), Africa, South America and North America.[21] Most notably is that the U.S. imports very little from the world's top producer of oil, Russia. The U.S. is the number 3 producer of oil in the world. The number one producer is Russia at 9.9 million barrels per day (MBD), Saudi Arabia at 9.7 and the U.S. coming in at 9.1 MBD.[22] This analysis provides an outlay of the supply and disbursement of oil around the world.

China ranks fourth behind Iran in crude oil production, which accounts for more than 5.4% of the world's crude oil consumption. However, China's output of approximately 189 million tons of oil does not meet half of its country's energy demands.[23] China's balances of supply and demand weigh more heavily towards demand. The U.S. supply and demand is less diverse. As previously noted, the U.S. is number 3 in oil production, and is number one in consumption. This means that the U.S. supplies 48.5% of its consumption while it imports 51.4% of consumption, or 9.67MBD, from oil exporting nations. [24] It is quite evident to see that the U.S. can and will be energy independent in the future.

It is interesting to see the trends oil supply and demand crossing paths between the U.S. and China. The U.S. has little or no involvement with Russia, while China has just signed a four pact energy agreement with the largest oil producers in the world. China's energy footprint is very relevant in the Middle East and in Africa. The U.S. remains the strategic superpower, security provider, and balancer in some of the key petroleum producing regions, most importantly the Persian Gulf.[25] By comparison and evidence, China is becoming or has become an important player in the Persian Gulf as well as many others, for good reason. It is apparent now that the U.S. and China's energy paths have crossed in the Middle East and in South America. The simple fact of this energy expansion ties back to China's rising economy and its exhausting demands for energy.

China's current economic condition is fairly stable. Early reports indicate for the year 2013 that China's economy will grow approximately 8.2% according to the Chinese Academy of Social Sciences (CASS), China's premier think tank.[26] This is up from the

7.7% growth estimated for 2012. Major growth in the economy according to CASS is in the area of expanding the fiscal deficit and cutting taxes that hinder economic efficiency.[27] The economic indicators of China's expanded growth are having an impact on the projected growth are pro-growth policies and investment in infrastructure construction. These are just a few of the indicators reflecting China's growth and continuous expansion.

With this approach for energy demands, supply and economic expansion, is there a counter argument against China's and its motives for economic expansion and energy security or will the resolution of this energy puzzle turn out to be a state of cooperation between the U.S. and China? One perspective from a Foreign Policy Research Institute analyst (the analyst) "is placing China in the historic perspective of a rising super power in the age of conflict over oil and other natural resources."[28]

The Chinese rule is still and will be Communist. With this political perspective, the analyst points out that "Chinese strategists might embrace a historical materialist account of the twentieth century."[29] The interpretation of this comment leads one to believe that Chinese strategists will look at the historical trends of rising superpowers, Japan, Germany, Russia and the U.S. since World War I, through to the Cold War period. These trends depicted these countries acquiring their oil requirements through wars, armed conflicts or the result of diplomatic shrewdness, as in the case with the U.S. and the Middle East after World War II and during the Cold War with Russia.

The analyst believes that China will approach their energy dilemma with three possible courses of action. The first, "China could trust that the free market in energy will continue to function. Second, China might pursue the military capability necessary to project power and secure its global energy supply lines. Third, call it the indirect approach-would be for China to defend its overseas energy supplies by disrupting hostile alliances and replacing them with a network of well-armed friends or client states along the routes."[30] All three courses of action do pose a viable choice for China to pursue, based on the historical trends of a rising superpower. China is much steeped in tradition and looks to the past to shape its current and future strategic objectives.

The first option of reliance on the international market, according to the Foreign Policy research Institute analyst, is not viable by current Chinese Communist Party standards. The analyst's opinion is based on documentation of Chinese Strategists and records of Chinese political and military attitudes. The second option of military power projection is also not viable. China knows it has limited military capabilities and would not be able to match the U.S. in its military capabilities. China's goal is to match the U.S. military capacity in roughly 30 years. Option 3 places China in a precarious situation. By blockading or denying access to key energy routes, China would be repeating the same paths taken by Japan and Germany which ultimately lead to a disruption in the world's oil supplies and ultimately war.

The opinions expressed by the Foreign Policy Research Institute does have some merit in that it allows the strategists and analysts to view this situation through a different lens. It paints a picture that makes the reader aware of each countries options, strengths, weaknesses and strategic thought process. China for example bases its strategic practices in the ancient writings of Sun Tzu in *the Art of War and* other "canonical Chinese works date to ancient China."[31] China is in a period of huge transition and is using its ancient writings and past world history to guide a form its future strategic goals. Conversely, what is not mentioned in this article is China's energy policy, its research in alternative and renewable fuel development and the ongoing unilateral discussion with the U.S. through military and diplomatic channels.

From this point, it appears that cooperation is a necessary tool to solve or at least mitigate the energy dilemma between the U.S. and China. No one nation can lay claim to all of the natural resource locations, production, development or distribution. Each country is reliant upon each other for either trade security; energy imports and exports.

The U.S. Energy Policy

Current U.S. policies towards China took root on January 3, 2012 during President Obama's Defense Strategy Guidance address to the Nation. The subject matter of the address outlined "Sustaining U.S. Global leadership: Priorities for the 21st Century." [32] The key focus of his address focused on the fiscal constraints the U.S. will be facing in the years to come and how the U.S. will have to refocus its fiscal challenges in meeting different demands around the world. He pointed out the resolution of the wars in the Middle East, specifically Iraq and Afghanistan. The address also focused on partnership, common interests, security, human rights, and global prosperity. A key component not articulated in his address dealt with the future of U.S. Energy security and policy.

In the March 30, 2011 document, "Blueprint for a Secure Energy Future," President Obama outlined three major strategies that will secure the U.S. in reaching its energy goals. They are to, "Develop and Secure America's Energy Supplies, Provide Consumers with Choices to Reduce Costs and Save Energy, and Innovate our Way to a Clean Energy Future." [33] President Obama stated in his blueprint, "The United States of America cannot afford to bet our long-term prosperity and security on a resource that

13

will eventually run out." [34] The thesis of this blueprint details how the U.S. will be a world leader, "by example" on energy conversation, clean energy and alternative fuel research and development, and cooperation with other countries in the world. As one of the worlds' technologically advanced nation, it is imperative that the U.S. uses its skills to advance the research and development of alternative and reusable fuel sources. With this in hand, U.S. policy can help shape and to another degree be a model for other countries to emulate.

The development and security of America's energy supplies strategy is focused on the lesser reliance of oil and coal for its future energy needs. Coupled with the increase in domestic oil and natural gas production, the U.S. is channeling its technology towards the safe development and exploration of natural resources and its search for alternative and reusable fuels. To encourage these practices, the U.S. government is rewarding the U.S. oil and gas companies for, "effectively and responsibly utilizing resources that belong to the American People."[35] The formula is quite simple; the U.S. is producing domestic oil and natural gas, the highest it's been since 2003, and by preserving this production domestically it is forcing the U.S. to develop alternate means of fuel. This will invariably lower the demand of oil and increase the demand for other forms of energy. With other forms of energy to choose from, comes a greater supply of choice and options.

The choice for reduced costs and saving energy is tied domestic transportation. "Transportation is the second costliest expense for most American households, and it's responsible for more than 70 percent of our petroleum consumption."[36] With the theme of this blueprint, the bottom line on this effort is the development and technological advance of fuel efficient vehicles. This strategy has a three pronged end state; create more transportation choices, lower dependency on oil and stimulate job growth in the U.S. manufacturing region.

Lastly, the U.S. and the rest of the world are in a race for developing clean energy. With clean energy comes the requirement of advanced technology and ingenuity. If any country in the world can develop this type of energy, harness it and apply it to domestic and governmental applications, they can effectively lessen their reliance on oil and natural gas, fossil fuels. The U.S. is well aware that this and realizes it won't' be easy to initiate. That is why President Obama in his 2011 State of the Union address proposed a new standard for America, "By 2035, we will generate 80 percent of our electricity from a diverse set of clean energy sources-including renewable energy sources like wind, solar, biomass, and hydropower."[37]

The China Energy Policy

China has made great progress in expanding its energy investment internally and externally. However, with its instability to balance its energy consumption with its fluctuating energy usage, it's unlikely that China will achieve a balanced energy security unless the energy reforms put in place by Beijing can stabilize its meteoric economic rise and subsequent duplicate rise in energy consumption.

China's energy security policies for the future appear to mirror that of the U.S. China too has become a more responsible economic superpower in that it realizes the impact its energy demands and consumption have on itself and the rest of the world.

As stated in China's Energy policy 2012, "To curb excessive consumption of energy resources and achieve the comprehensive, balanced and sustainable development of the economy, society and ecology, China keeps strengthening its efforts

15

in energy conservation and emission reduction, and strives to raise the efficiency of energy utilization."[38] The content of this statement did not come from an outsider's perspective of China's energy policy. It was pulled directly from The Information Office of the State Council in China. This comment is a self critique of China's current and future needs for a safe, economically stable, and cleaner energy future. Contrary to the belief that China is not trying to cater to the needs of its people, China is providing for its society. China/Beijing realizes that in order to have a stable economy, it must ensure its populations is safe and stable as well. One element of the society feeds the other.

China's energy security policy includes, but is not limited to energy conservation, development in non-fossil fuel energy, advances in science and technology and developing programs for environmental conservation. Coincidently, the U.S. is also striving to achieve these similar goals in the next 20 to 25 years. The only difference between the two countries is that the U.S. will most likely achieve it strategic goals faster. China's main challenge in this area is it needs to develop its economy while meeting the demands of high energy consumption. The U.S. does not face this daunting challenge.

One other major difference between the U.S. and China is China's increasing demand for imported energy sources in the last few years. On the other hand, the U.S. reliance on foreign energy sources has decreased. This of course is due to high domestic oil and LNG production, high strategic petroleum reserves and the increasing use of alternative fuel sources. China unlike the U.S. does not possess a high store of energy reserves nor does it have an emergency capability to respond to an energy crisis based on the fluctuating international energy market prices.

A major strategic weakness in China's energy requirements is its reliance on maritime and pipeline deliverance systems. Critical maritime choke points for China's flow of imports for crude oil are through the Strait of Malacca, Strait of Hormuz, the Suez Canal and the Turkish Straits. The riskiest choke point is the Strait of Malacca, second only to the Strait of Hormuz. It is a narrow channel and shortest transport route between the Persian Gulf and East Asia through to the South China. A land "chokepoint" for China lies within its own boundaries. Currently China transports 80 percent of its coal for power via rail. [39] The issue is that 45 percent of the total Chinese rail system is for coal transport, but only two are dedicated for coal transport. The rest is shared between passenger and cargo rail systems.

What does this all mean to China and its energy future? It is not bleak, but it will be major challenge. China has t overcome many obstacles in international energy competition, levels of productivity and development, the country's irrational industrial structure and energy mix, extensive development and use of energy resources and sluggish reform of relevant systems and mechanisms. From the words of the Chinese cabinet, ""China did not, does not, and will not pose any threat to the world's energy security."[40] China is on a quest to reform its energy practices. It realizes that it cannot conquer this task alone. It along with the other natural resource dependant nations will, "strive to maintain stability of the international energy market and energy prices, secure the international energy routes and make due contributions to safeguarding international energy security."[41]

Conflict/Cooperation between U.S. and China

China is developing its domestic capabilities of natural resources to counter its import demands for LNG, oil and other petroleum products. China appears to be building its house on the inside, taking care of its domestic priorities in order to stabilize its economic and international requirements. It is building a sound foundation. These developments and accelerated moves for resource expansion and development can be signals to the world that China is making strides in natural energy resources. The world is certainly anxious to see if China will meet its objectives with responsibilities.

With its clean energy incentive and program, the U.S. is targeted to become" a global leader in developing and manufacturing cutting-edge clean energy technologies."[42] This coincides directly with the BP commentary and prediction that the U.S., specifically North America will be energy independent by 2030 and that China and India will remain energy dependant. However, China has turned to shale gas exploration within its own boundaries. The basic necessity for this was domestic usage and trade. Currently China's demand is outweighing its supply for natural gas and relies heavily on imports. Hence the energy pact agreements made with Russia recently have provided a "bridging " for energy security for China until it is able to capitalize on its own natural resources. Experts predict that by the year 2020, China could be able to cut its demand for Liquid Natural Gas (LNG).[43] Australia's Macquarie Bank in September 2010 also predicted that the Chinese expansion and development of natural gas and the Russian pipeline projects are a risk to Australian exports of LNG to China.[44] China is smart; it is not relying on one type of energy, delivery system or country for its energy needs.

With that being said, China's energy dependence will not wane any time soon. The U.S. will not have to deal with a China that gives up its demands for any types of energy. Although China is, like the U.S. instituting energy programs for the advancement of clean fuel, alternative fuels, renewable energy and an overall greener environment, the bottom line is, "Worldwide, fossil energy, including coal and oil will continue to play a dominant role in energy supply for a long time to come."[45] The checks and balances of energy security have the U.S. Congress reporting on the developments and inner workings of the Chinese government and its energy policies.

The U.S. Congress has drawn major implications, conclusions, and recommendations dealing with China's expansion on natural resource development and procurement. The initial implication cited by the Congressional report dealt with China's "immense capacity to produce and consume raw materials, driving both supply and demand for several global commodities."[46] This has a negative and positive effect on the global economy. To point out, China is investing heavily in the U.S. shale gas development boosting projects and increasing exports. Conversely, the U.S. as well as other countries is reliant upon China for minerals and mineral products. This creates uncertainty in the markets, not to mention political instability.

China's advantage over the U.S. in resource control and attainment is superior. The edge lies within China's huge economic power. China's state owned oil companies are under the control of the government. Beijing provides political and financial support and guidance that enhances companies' competitiveness, allowing them to invest in high risk ventures and overpay in their fields for attractive assets in North America and elsewhere.[47] Since China has the means to "buy into" its resource needs, the U.S. competitive edge in energy development and production is seen as weakening. Since oil companies are not under the control or direction of the U.S. government, the U.S. needs to find a way to counter China's immense "pocketbook".

The U.S. either develops marketable alternative, renewable energy sources that China cannot compete with, or develop policy that prevents or precludes China from using the U.S. reliance of minerals as a political tool. This fear has merit. China did actually withhold rare materials over a diplomatic dispute with Japan. The U.S. cannot stand idly by and let China or any other country with indigenous raw materials dictate the political and economic climate. Structure and cooperation of resource allocation, development and production must be of paramount priority for all to survive.

In one of Congress's conclusions, it cited that China's Achilles heel in the energy resource game lies within its foreign dependence on energy. This is viewed by China's leaders as a "strategic vulnerability."[48] It imports oil from unstable nation states (such as Iran, Sudan, and South Sudan). Coupled with the unstable region, China also fears its maritime trade routes such as the Straits of Hormuz and the Straits of Malacca as trade route chokepoints. China's biggest fear is the U.S.'s capability to blockade these chokepoints. China's energy shipment, which is over 80% of its imported oil, goes through the Straits of Malacca.[49] What this fear has led Beijing to do is to diversify its reliance's on foreign energy and trade routes.

Congress also concluded from its report that Africa is a continent that China has diversified its efforts towards in the search for new and developing energy. The relationship between China and Africa goes far beyond natural resource excavation. Granted, China imports about one-fourth of crude oil originating in sub-Saharan Africa and more than two-thirds of Africa's exports to China consist of crude oil.[50] China's interests with Africa also lay in their infrastructure, education, and information technology. This not only benefits Africa, but also trade partners around the world.

The threat between the U.S. and China regarding energy consumption and energy claims is not a point of contention in this region. The U.S. does give aid to Africa, in 2009; it gave $8 billion in assistance to Africa, while China gave an estimated $1.4 billion. [51] The relationship between the U.S. and Africa is very stable. This area/region of the world is not of growing concern for the U.S. and China regarding energy issues. The U.S. interest with Africa lie within the supporting public health programs, democratization efforts, counterterrorism cooperation, the development of health infrastructure, and improved regulatory institutions.

Congress outlined that China has "significant energy interests in North, Central, and Southeast Asia. North America has emerged as the top destination for Chinese energy investments in recent years."[52] This neatly ties back to the comments made in the BP report that by the year 2030, North America, notably the U.S., will be energy independent as opposed to China and India.

The recommendations cited by the commission in the 2012 Report to Congress recognize the vulnerabilities that both the U.S. and China have in this energy "conflict." The establishment of an interagency task force with the secretaries of Commerce, Defense, Energy and Interior, and State along with the director of the U.S. Geological Survey to, "develop a government wide definition and list of "critical minerals, and develop a plan regarding those minerals to reduce the vulnerability of the U.S. to pressure from China or any other country for political or economic advantage."[53] The "soft" approach Congress is recommending is using the (Diplomacy, Information, Military and Economic (DIME) model) of the U.S. National Strategy. Other recommendations included the necessity of transatlantic dialogue between members of

Congress and others using the "Transatlantic Policy Network or the Transatlantic Legislators Dialogue to promote the discussion of economic, political, and security issues as they relate to China and Asia."[54] These recommendations alone stand testament that the U.S. Congress is taking a hardnosed position on the dangers and insecurities of China's energy expansion.

China as a growing superpower has to learn how to manage its internal and external relations with other nations over resource allocation. Continued misuse of natural resources and balancing the growing economy, could still ignite conflicts within the South China Sea and the Middle East. This provocation by China has been seen already in the South China Sea with the littoral states. China will continue its expansion and territorial claims to exercise its perceived right over natural resources and territory.

China is not a nation historically known for its aggression or occupying tenets. Historically, it has been an isolationist country. Only now in the last 15-20 years has China realized its potential and place in the international order. China has found itself as an emerging power in transition. It must learn and with the assistance of the U.S. will become a valued and responsible partner and ally in all aspects of international matters.

Conclusion

The energy puzzle between the U.S. and China is shaping up to be a slowly building relationship on trust, mutual understanding, open communication and healthy competitiveness. However, "there is a desperate need for a confidence building process."[55] Based on China's strategic/military doctrine, it does not appear that they are poised or have a desire for an armed conflict with the U.S. over rights to natural resources. Their struggles over terrorism, piracy, regional security and stabilization are of utmost importance not only with themselves, but with the U.S. and its Asian Pacific

22

partner states. Regional stability is the cornerstone that will drive economic growth and peaceful expansion.

With the meteoric rise of China's economy and dependence on natural resources over the last 30 plus years, it has been quite evident that there have not been any major regional or international conflicts between the U.S. and China. Since September 11, 2001 the U.S. and China "Have effectively collaborated to solve or manage regional and global threats and challenges."[56] Their collaboration has included such efforts as counter-terrorism measures, nuclear proliferation efforts again North Korea and pandemic issues such as SARS in 2003 and later the avian flu. Common human domain issues are paramount to cultivating any type of a mutual interest relationship. Energy security should be no different.

The roadmap to a cooperative and viable solution for global energy security is a tenable, trust building system of near and short term objectives set by each country. The implication of this means that the U.S. and China must in no small measure become role models for the rest of the world. "The issue is not cooperation on better U.S.-China relations for its own sake but cooperation that addresses our vital and common interests in energy on a global basis."[57] Common interests, differences in policy, shared responsibilities and mutual understandings are all key components that go into working out differences and coming to resolutions. Diplomacy and communication is key for these to carry on for now and the future.

To illustrate growing cooperation between the two countries, China's biggest hindrance in developing its shale gas resources is its current "above ground" infrastructure and expertise to develop this product commercially. China has partnered with the U.S. to assist them in their pursuit of clean economically viable shale gas production. This agreement of information sharing was launched in November 2009 between President Obama and President Hu and was called the "U.S.-China Shale Gas Resource Initiative."[58] This initiative allowed the U.S. to share its experiences and assessments on how it capitalized on the development and production of shale gas in the U.S. This cooperation would lead China to accelerate its production of Shale gas safely and better economically. Another example towards the road to worldwide energy security is the development of, "a public-private partnership to promote joint commercial ventures."[59] This venture allows Chinese investors to invest in wind technology in the U.S. while creating employment in this field for U.S. citizens.

If China and the U.S. can show resolve or healthy competition over the energy puzzle, it would only seem fit that the other nations in the world would fall into place and understand the compliance that exists between the two superpowers. Part of this is to agree that we will disagree on many issues and try to prevent them from becoming toxic in the larger relationship.[60] One element of this communication piece is to ensure that the current posture of national competition over energy and its reserves is postured towards an aggressive commercial competition[61]. This will redirect the U.S. and China's focus on energy security from being an inward unilateral competition to a bi-lateral healthy competition and will spur common energy interests.

Partnerships, initiatives or simple actions like this between the U.S. and China is an indicator to believe that there is mutual respect for each countries power and weaknesses and that fostering growth and sharing in bilateral issues and interests can only lead to clean energy growth, security and prosperity between the two countries.

Endnotes

[1] David Lai., *"The United States and China in Power Transition."* (Carlisle, PA Department of Strategic Studies Institute),.47

[2] Leon E. Panetta, *Annual Report to Congress –Military and Security Developments Involving the People's Republic of China–2012* (Washington, DC: U.S. Department of Defense, May 2012), 2

[3] Mikkal Herberg, "China's Energy Rise and the Future of US China Energy Relations," June 21, 2011, http://newamerica.net/publications/policy/china_s_energy_rise_and_the_future_of_us_china_energy_relations (accessed January 16, 2013)

[4] BP Statistical Review of World Energy- June 2012 http://www.bp.com/assets/bp_internet/globalbp/globalbp_uk_english/reports_and_publications/statistical_energy_review_2011/STAGING/local_assets/pdf/statistical_review_of_world_energy_full_report_2012.pdfBP (accessed January 10, 2013)

[5] Elizabeth C. Economy ed., "China's Energy Future, An Introductory Comment," July-August 2011, http://www.cfr.org/china/chinas-energy-future-introductory-comment/p25633 (accessed, 30 October 2012)

[6] Ibid.

[7] Panetta on New U.S. Defense Strategy, Asia-Pacific Policy". June 2, 2012, http://www.uspolicy.be/headline/panetta-new-us-defense--strategy-asia-pacific-policy (accessed October 30, 2012

[8] US Energy Information Administration, International Energy Outlook 2011, September 19, 2011 http://www.eia.gov/forecasts/ieo (accessed January 10, 2013)

[9] Christof Ruhl, BP Statistical Review of World Energy- June 2012, Energy Outlook 2030, video file, http://www.bp.com/extendedsectiongenericarticle.do?categoryId=9048887&contentId=7082549 (accessed January 10, 2013)

[10] People's Daily Online, "China's oil production ranks 4th in world, only meets half domestic demand," February 9, 2010 http://english.peopledaily.com.cn/90001/90778/90860/6891500.html (accessed January 29, 2013)

[11] U.S. Joint Forces Command, *The Joint Operating Environment, - 2010*, (Suffolk, VA: U.S. Joint Forces Command, March 15, 2010), 19.

[12] Travis Hioum., "China becoming dependant on Foreign Oil," December 7, 2012, http://www.fool.com/investing/general/2012/12/07/china-becoming-dependent-on-foreign-oil.aspx (accessed Dec 9, 2012)

[13] Mikkal Herberg, "China's Energy Rise and the Future of US China Energy Relations," June 21, 2011, http://newamerica.net/publications/policy/china_s_energy_rise_and_the_future_of_us_china_energy_relations (accessed January 16, 2013)

[14] Ibid.

[15] Panetta on New U.S. Defense Strategy, Asia-Pacific Policy". June 2, 2012, http://www.uspolicy.be/headline/panetta-new-us-defense--strategy-asia-pacific-policy (accessed October 30, 2012

[16] US Energy Information Administration, International Energy Outlook 2011, September 19, 2011, http://www.eia.gov/forecasts/ieo (accessed January 10, 2013)

[17] U.S. Congress, Senate, 2012 Report to Congress of the, *US-China Economic Security Review Commission,* 112th Cong., 2nd sess., November 2012, 329.

[18] Xinhua, "China, Russia Inking Four Agreements on Energy Cooperation," December 6, 2012, http://europe.chinadaily.com.cn/business/2012-12/06/content_15991674.htm (accessed December 9, 2012)

[19] Ibid.

[20] Steven Mufson, "The Coal Killer," *The Washington Post*, November 25, 2012

[21] Charles Hughes Smith, "We're Number 1 (and No.3) Surprising Facts About the U.S. and Oil," http://www.dailyfinance.com/2011/02/28/surprising-facts-about-us-and-oil (accessed January 29, 2013)

[22] Ibid.

[23] People's Daily Online, "China's oil production ranks 4th in world, only meets half domestic demand," February 9, 2010 http://english.peopledaily.com.cn/90001/90778/90860/6891500.html (accessed January 29, 2013)

[24] Charles Hughes Smith, "We're Number 1 (and No.3) Surprising Facts About the U.S. and Oil," http://www.dailyfinance.com/2011/02/28/surprising-facts-about-us-and-oil (accessed January 29, 2013)

[25] Mikkal Herberg, "China's Energy Rise and the Future of US China Energy Relations," June 21, 2011, http://newamerica.net/publications/policy/china_s_energy_rise_and_the_future_of_us_china_energy_relations (accessed January 16, 2013)

[26] Xiaoyi Shao and Lucy Hornby, "China Economy May Grow 8.2% in 2013," December 4, 2012, http://news.yahoo.com/china-economy-may-grow-8-2-percent-2013-033839091--business.html (accessed December 5, 2012)

[27] Ibid.

[28] Jacqueline N. Neal, "China and the Politics of Oil," May 2012, http://www.fpri.org/enotes/2012/201205.deal.china-politics-oil.pdf (accessed January 29, 2013)

[29] Ibid.

[30] Ibid.

[31] Ibid.

[32] Barack H. Obama, *National Defense Strategy*, (Washington, DC: The White House, 3 January 2012)

[33] Barack H. Obama, *Blueprint for a Secure Energy Future*, (Washington, DC: The White House 30 March 2011), http://www.whitehouse.gov/sites/default/files/blueprint_secure_energy_future.pdf., (accessed January 17, 2013)

[34] Ibid

[35] Ibid

[36] Ibid

[37] Ibid

[38] China.org.cn., "China's Energy Conditions and Policies," December 26, 2007., http://www.china.org.cn/english/environment/236955.htm (accessed January 20, 2013)

[39] Jenny Lin, ed., "China's Energy Security Dilemma," http://project2049.net/documents/china_energy_dilemma_lin.pdf, (accessed November 7, 2012)

[40] China.org.cn., "China's Energy Conditions and Policies," December 26, 2007., http://www.china.org.cn/english/environment/236955.htm (accessed January 20, 2013)

[41] Ibid.

[42] Ibid.

[43] Jane Nakano, David Pumphrey, Robert Price, Jr., Molly A. Walton, "Prospects for Shale Gas Development in Asia, Examining Potentials and Challenges in China and India," August 2012, http://csis.org/publication/prospects-shale-gas-development-asia (accessed November 7, 2012)

[44] Ibid.

[45] China.org.cn., "China's Energy Conditions and Policies," December 26, 2007., http://www.china.org.cn/english/environment/236955.htm (accessed January 20, 2013)

[46] U.S. Congress, Senate, 2012 Report to Congress of the, *US-China Economic Security Review Commission,* 112th Cong., 2nd sess., November 2012, 362.

[47] Ibid., 362

[48] Ibid., 362

[49] U.S. Joint Forces Command, *The Joint Operating Environment, - 2010*, (Suffolk, VA: U.S. Joint Forces Command, March 15, 2010), 41.

[50] Shimelse Ali and Nida Jafrani., eds., "China's Growing Role in Africa: Myths and Facts," February 10, 2012, http://carnegieendowment.org/ieb/2012/02/09/china-s-growing-role-in-africa-myths-and-facts/9j54, (accessed November 7, 2012)

[51] Ibid.

[52] U.S. Congress, Senate, 2012 Report to Congress of the, *US-China Economic Security Review Commission,* 112th Cong., 2nd sess., November 2012, 363.

[53] Ibid., 364

[54] Ibid., 364

[55] Mikkal Herberg, "China's Energy Rise and the Future of US China Energy Relations," June 21, 2011, http://newamerica.net/publications/policy/china_s_energy_rise_and_the_future_of_us_china_energy_relations (accessed January 16, 2013)

[56] Richard Holbrooke and Vishakha Desai., eds. "A Roadmap for US-China Cooperation on Energy and Climate Change," February 2009, http://www.c2es.org/publications/us-china-roadmap-energy-climate-cooperation, (accessed January 17, 2013)

[57] Ibid.

[58] U.S. Joint Forces Command, *The Joint Operating Environment, - 2010*, (Suffolk, VA: U.S. Joint Forces Command, March 15, 2010), 24.

[59] Steven Chu, "US-China Clean Energy Cooperation; A Progress Report by the US Department of Energy", January 2011, http://www.us-china-cerc.org/pdfs/US_China_Clean_Energy_Progress_Report.pdf, (accessed January 31, 2013)

[60] Richard Holbrooke and Vishakha Desai., eds. "A Roadmap for US-China Cooperation on Energy and Climate Change," February 2009, http://www.c2es.org/publications/us-china-roadmap-energy-climate-cooperation, (accessed January 17, 2013)

[61] Ibid.

www.ingramcontent.com/pod-product-compliance
Lightning Source LLC
Chambersburg PA
CBHW080801290526
45790CB00008B/3536